畅学英语听说教程

下册

主　编　乔秀平　李芳玲
副主编　孙　霞　王广英　褚冉冉　张　娟
　　　　高　蕾　李红颖　林　岩

北京理工大学出版社
BEIJING INSTITUTE OF TECHNOLOGY PRESS

版权专有 侵权必究

图书在版编目（CIP）数据

畅学英语听说教程：下册 / 乔秀平, 李芳玲主编. -- 北京：北京理工大学出版社，2022.1（2024.1重印）
ISBN 978-7-5763-0810-5

Ⅰ.①畅… Ⅱ.①乔…②李… Ⅲ.①英语 – 听说教学 – 高等职业教育 – 教材 Ⅳ.①H319.9

中国版本图书馆CIP数据核字（2022）第004880号

责任编辑：武丽娟　　**文案编辑**：武丽娟
责任校对：刘亚男　　**责任印制**：施胜娟

出版发行 / 北京理工大学出版社有限责任公司
社　　址 / 北京市丰台区四合庄路6号
邮　　编 / 100070
电　　话 / （010）68914026（教材售后服务热线）
　　　　　（010）68944437（课件资源服务热线）
网　　址 / http://www.bitpress.com.cn

版 印 次 / 2024年1月第1版第2次印刷
印　　刷 / 河北盛世彩捷印刷有限公司
开　　本 / 787 mm×1092 mm　1/16
印　　张 / 8
字　　数 / 112千字
定　　价 / 39.00元

图书出现印装质量问题，请拨打售后服务热线，负责调换

编写说明
WRITE INSTRUCTIONS

《畅学英语听说教程》共 10 个单元，分上下两册，供高职一年级使用。

编写原则

本教材以教育部 2021 年颁发的《高等职业教育专科英语课程标准》为依据，以二十大报告中"落实立德树人根本任务""弘扬劳动精神、奋斗精神、奉献精神、创造精神、勤俭节约精神""增强文化自信"等重要论述为指导编写而成。教材编写紧紧围绕"职业"理念，以促进学生英语学科核心素养的发展为目的，以培养学生职场涉外沟通能力、多元文化交流能力、语言思维提升能力和自主学习完善能力为目标，为高职院校的专业、行业教学服务，为学生的职业发展及终身学习服务。

教材特色

本教材兼顾时代性、实用性和趣味性，教材编排具有以下特点：

1. 版式设计个性化

教材的编写秉承"学生自主学习为主，教师引导为辅"和"学生知识的自我构建"的工学结合核心理念，以"活页教材"的形式呈现，采用"学习素材＋学习导航＋活页笔记＋学习评价"四位一体的版面设计，实现和指导学生的自主思维，帮助学生应对职场交际，适应职业需求。

2. 素材要素多样化

教材将语音、话题、场景、任务、活动和中华优秀文化等多个要素有机融合，语料真实新颖，兼顾生活和职业场景，场景与任务多样化，语言复现率高。

3. 情景练习真实化

教材贯穿"学中用，用中学"的理念，用真实的职场情境任务推动学生的语言学习，在加强语言基础知识和基本技能训练的同时，着重培养学生的职场英语实用能力，既体现职业教育重视操作的特点，也符合职业学校学生喜爱实践的个性。

4. 单元主题职场化

教材根据新课标的课程目标要求，编写了与职场话题相关的十个专题，构成职业与个人、职业与社会和职业与环境三个主题模块，每个模块均融入中华优秀文化，渗透课程思政的理念。

内容构成

本教材的每个单元围绕一个专题编写，共分为七大板块：

学习目标（Learning Focus）：该板块明确列出了各单元在语音、听力、口语训练和中国优秀文化传播方面的学习目标和需要掌握的学习重点，使学习过程有的放矢，学习效果评估有据可依。

乐学英语（Enjoying English）：该部分设计了语音练习，注重实用性的同时兼顾趣味性；提供了谚语和绕口令，使学生既能强化语音训练，又能丰富文化知识，提高人文素养；英文歌曲部分使学生在学习之余进行放松，同时体会语言学习的乐趣与美妙。

听力训练（Testing Your Ears）：本板块内容的编排依据单元主题精选对话素材，以填词、填短语、填句子的方式由易到难，循序渐进。以听为基础，先听再说，难度递增，使学生能就日常话题和职业相关话题进行有效的交谈。

口语训练（Talking Together）：本环节采用任务教学的形式，以小组或班级活动为主，锻炼学生的口语能力以及团队合作中的沟通能力。

职场训练（Training Task）：本环节设计真实的交际场景，让学生在熟悉听说对话的基础上，自编对话，实现听说的自然衔接，完成职场交流，培养学生职场通用英语的运用能力。

中国故事（China Story）：该板块精选中国故事，让学生以自述或情景剧方式再现故事内容，旨在增强文化自信，传播中华优秀文化。

检查清单（Checklist）：此环节旨在培养学生自主学习与自我管理能力，帮助学生回顾与总结每单元学习的内容，检查学习目标是否达成；各学习小组成员之间可以互相查看与共享，促进个人与团队成长，提升学习效果。

建议各院校根据实际需要有选择地使用本教材。本教材配有网络课程，课程网址为：https://mooc1-1.chaoxing.com/course-ans/ps/222083908.

目录
CONTENTS

Unit 1　Workplace Routine ·· 001

Unit 2　Working Environment ·· 023

Unit 3　Output Quality ·· 049

Unit 4　Employment Security ·· 073

Unit 5　Social Responsibility ··· 095

1

Unit 1

Workplace Routine

Learning Focus

单元内容	Enjoying English	1）强读与弱读 2）押韵 3）名言与绕口令 4）歌曲：*I Have a Dream* 我有一个梦
	Testing Your Ears	1）通勤方式 2）工作预约 3）请假
	Talking Together	1）安排宾馆入住 2）工作压力
	Training Task	1）请假 2）入住宾馆
	China Story	*Confucius Climbed Mount Tai* 孔子登泰山
单元目标	语言知识目标	能够用英语描述职场日常
	语言技能目标	1）能够听懂与职场日常相关的对话 2）能够用英语谈论职场日常
	学习策略	迅速捕捉大意，创设情景，通过对话和反思进行合作学习
	情感态度	培养严谨的工作态度和积极的生活态度
	文化意识	讲中国故事，传播儒家文化，增强民族自豪感
	职业素养	培养自我管理和主动调适的能力

Task 1 Enjoying English

Strong and Weak Reading

任务内容	听录音，找出弱读词
任务目的	准确把握句子中的强读与弱读
任务形式	听，回答，跟读
训练技能	句子的节奏感和韵律感

Directions: *Articles, some prepositions, pronouns and conjunctions are usually not stressed in phrases and expressions. Underline these words. Each expression will be read twice.*

1. go to school
2. nice and comfortable
3. easy but boring
4. interested in reading
5. look at me
6. not at all
7. a cup of tea
8. far from home
9. more or less
10. step by step

Part 2

Rhyme

任务内容	听录音，选出与所听到的词押韵的单词
任务目的	体会英语语言的韵律
任务形式	听，回答，小组讨论
训练技能	听音、辨音能力

Directions: Two words rhyme when the last sounds of the words are the same, like "she and key" and "late and eight". You will hear some words and decide which of the four words in the group rhymes with the word you hear. After you have chosen the best answer, repeat what you hear. Each word will be read twice.

1. A. know   B. now   C. raw   D. saw
2. A. bit   B. caught   C. nut   D. right
3. A. read   B. rat   C. rate   D. red
4. A. seem   B. strict   C. meet   D. mind
5. A. beer   B. bear   C. fear   D. fire
6. A. loose   B. lose   C. rise   D. rose
7. A. gone   B. long   C. ton   D. tone
8. A. call   B. full   C. girl   D. tool
9. A. sigh   B. spare   C. brain   D. bring
10. A. ask   B. best   C. haste   D. must

Part 3

Proverbs and Tongue Twisters

（1）Proverbs

任务内容	学习名言警句
任务目的	从名言中获得启迪
任务形式	熟读，背诵
训练技能	启智增慧

Directions: Read the following proverbs after the recording and practice more by yourself.

A friend in need is a friend indeed.
患难见真情。

A little learning is a dangerous thing.
一知半解，害人不浅。

All's well that ends well.
结果好就是好。

East or west, home is best.
金窝银窝不如自己的草窝。

Seeing is believing.
眼见为实。

（2）Tongue twister

任务内容	练习绕口令
任务目的	纠正发音，提升口语流利度
任务形式	自主练习，小组竞赛
训练技能	听音、辨音和发音能力

Directions: Read the following tongue twister after the recording and practice more by yourself.

A flea and a fly in a flue got caught, so what'd they do?

一只跳蚤和一只苍蝇在烟道里被困住了，它们会做什么？

"Let us flee!" said the fly.

"让我们逃吧！"苍蝇说。

"Let us fly!" said the flea.

"让我们飞吧！"跳蚤说。

So they flew through a flaw in the flue.

就这样，它们从烟道里的一条裂纹处飞跑了。

Enjoy Yourself

Directions: Listen to the song and sing along.

I Have a Dream 我有一个梦

I have a dream, a song to sing

我有一个梦，一首想唱的歌

To help me cope with anything

帮助我对抗一切

If you see the wonder of a fairy tale

如果你见过童话的神奇

You can take the future even if you fail
你就可以掌握未来，纵然是失败

I believe in angels
我相信有天使

Something good in everything I see
我所看见的一切都是美好的

I believe in angels
我相信有天使

When I know the time is right for me
当我知道时机来临

I'll cross the stream
我将涉水过溪

I have a dream
因为我有一个梦

I have a dream, a fantasy
我有一个梦，一个幻想

To help me through reality
帮助我熬过现实

And my destination makes it worth the while
我的目的使这一切都没有白费

Pushing through the darkness still another mile
穿过黑暗仍有很长的路要走

I believe in angels
我相信有天使

Something good in everything I see
我所看见的一切都是美好的

I believe in angels
我相信有天使

When I know the time is right for me

当我知道时机来临

I'll cross the stream

我将涉水过溪

I have a dream

因为我有一个梦

I have a dream, a song to sing

我有一个梦，一首想唱的歌

To help me cope with anything

帮助我对抗一切

If you see the wonder of a fairy tale

如果你见过童话的神奇

You can take the future even if you fail

你就可以掌握未来，纵然是失败

I believe in angels

我相信有天使

Something good in everything I see

我所看见的一切都是美好的

I believe in angels

我相信有天使

When I know the time is right for me

当我知道时机来临

I'll cross the stream

我将涉水过溪

I have a dream

因为我有一个梦

I'll cross the stream

我将涉水过溪

I have a dream

因为我有一个梦

Task 2 Testing Your Ears

New Words

commute	v./n.	通勤
pack	v.	挤满
squish	v.	压扁；压坏
drawback	n.	缺点
release	v.	解除；减轻
brief	v.	向……介绍情况
account	n.	报告
Chop Suey	n.	中式菜
exhausted	adj.	筋疲力尽的

Commuting

任务内容	关于通勤方式的对话
任务目的	学会用英语讨论不同的通勤方式
任务形式	听，填词
职场技能	合理选择出行方式

Directions: Listen to the following dialogue twice and fill in the blanks.

A: I can't wait until my car is repaired. The commuting with public transportation is killing me.

B: It can't be that bad.

A: But it is! Take this morning for example. The (1)_____ was so packed this morning. I got totally squished by about a hundred busy (2)_____ on the way to work.

B: At least the subway is better than the bus. It's faster for one thing. And usually less (3)_____. But the drawback is that the subway is more expensive than the bus. It adds up over time if you take it every day.

A: That's true. The bus is even worse. Just thinking about taking the bus every day makes me tired! Hey, how do you get to work every day?

B: I ride my bike. I don't live too far away, so it's pretty (4)_____. It's only about a ten-minute bike ride from my house to the office.

A: I'll bet it's good exercise, too...a good way to keep fit.

B: Yes, not only a good way to keep in shape, but a good way to relieve (5)_____ as well. While you're stressed out by your commute, I'm releasing all the stress of the day with mine.

Part 2

Appointment

任务内容	关于工作预约的对话
任务目的	学会用英语预约时间，商讨工作
任务形式	听，填短语
职场技能	养成事前预约意识

Directions: Listen to the following dialogue twice and fill in the blanks.

A: Excuse me, Don? I hate to bother you, but I need your help on something. Do you have time to brief me on the Martin account today?

B: Oh, that's right. You are supposed to (1)_____ on that account tomorrow. I know there are some things I need to share with you about that. But, gosh, I don't know. Things are really busy for me today. The only time I can manage to (2)_____ might be over lunch break.

A: I hate to make you work through your lunch break with how busy you are.

B: It's okay... I've already had several days in a row working through lunch.

A: How about this? We can make it (3) _____ this afternoon, and I'll order some Chinese food for delivery. It'll be my treat.

B: You don't have to do that.

A: I insist. I really appreciate you taking the time to work me in. What is your favorite fast food? I'll (4)_____ your taste.

B: Actually I do like Chinese... Let's (5) _____ for Chop Suey and the Martin account at about 12:30. Does that sound good?

A: Great. I'll bring the food.

Part 3

Asking for Leave

任务内容	关于请假的对话
任务目的	学会用英语请假
任务形式	听，填句子
职场技能	恰当合理地表达个人诉求

Directions: Listen to the following dialogue twice and fill in the blanks.

A: Mr. Black, (1)_____. I've been feeling exhausted these days.

B: That's no problem. Let me see... You still have ten days annual leave left, is that right?

A: Yes. I was wondering if I could take another two weeks off.

B: That's long leave. (2)_____?

A: The project I'm in charge of now will be done by the end of this week. I'd like to take my leave from next Monday on.

B: Well, all right. (3)_____.

A: Thank you, Mr. Black. There are no immediate projects coming up at the moment. (4)_____. He is taking part in several projects as my assistant and knows how to maintain relationships with our clients.

B: Great! (5)_____.

A: I will. Many thanks, Mr. Black.

Task 3　Talking Together

New Words

confirmation	n.	确认
initial	n.	首字母
pushy	adj.	咄咄逼人的
deadline	n.	截止日期
continental breakfast	n.	欧陆式早餐

Part 1

Check-in

任务内容	关于安排宾馆入住的对话
任务目的	学会用英语沟通入住
任务形式	角色扮演
职场技能	良好的接待与沟通能力

Conversation 1:

Directions: *Complete the following dialogue according to the hints given in Chinese and role-play it with your partner.*

A: Hello, welcome to Prise Star Hotel. May I help you?

B: Hi, yes, I (1) _____ (有预定). My secretary

called and booked a room a couple of weeks ago. The reservation should be for (2)_____ （双人床）, non-smoking room.

A: And what name was the reservation made under?

B: It should be under Steve Johnson.

A: Mmm, let me see. It seems there is no Johnson listed for a room for tonight. Is there any other name that your reservation may be listed under?

B: No. Here is the confirmation number. Would that help? It's 898007. I had the room booked with a Visa card.

A: Ah, yes, here it is. You have a standard double room, non-smoking on the 3rd floor. I just need to see some identification and the credit card you booked the room with if you don't mind.

B: Sure, here it is. Would it be possible to (3)_____ （退房） and pay the bill in the morning. Also, what time is breakfast served?

A: There is a continental breakfast buffet from 6:00 a.m. to 10:00 a.m.. It's in the lobby. Also you can (4)_____ （结账） in the morning, but we require a 20% deposit upfront. But I can just (5)_____ （记录） of your credit card on file. OK, I've got you all set up if you could just sign here, and initial here. Here is your room key. Anything else I can do for you?

B: Yes, could you call me a taxi please?

A: OK.

Part 2

Career Pressure

任务内容	关于工作压力的对话
任务目的	学会用英语讨论工作中的压力
任务形式	角色扮演
职场技能	应对压力，自我调适能力

Conversation 2:

Directions: Place the following sentences in correct order to form a dialogue and role-play it with your partner.

a. I'm under a lot of pressure.

b. Take it easy and say something to me if you like.

c. I stayed up last night.

d. Is there anything I can do for you?

e. You look so concerned!

A: John, you look pale. What happened?

B: (1) _____

A: Did you have something on your mind? (2) _____

   Maybe I can help you!

B: Well, (3) _____

   My manager is very pushy. He assigned
   me two projects. Now the deadlines are
   near but I have finished neither of them.

A: (4)

B: Well, I guess no one can help me but myself. For the moment, I just need someone to talk to so that I can relieve my stress.

A: I know your feeling. (5)_____

B: Oh, buddy, you are so kind. Thank you!

A: Not at all!

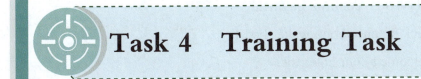

Task 4　Training Task

任务内容	1）请假 2）安排宾馆入住
任务目的	能够用英语沟通请假与入住事宜
任务形式	角色扮演
职场技能	良好的沟通能力

Directions: Make dialogues for the following situations. You can refer to the words, expressions and patterns given below.

Situation 1: Suppose you are Li Lei from ABC Company, and you would like to talk with Peter, your boss, to take some time off. Make a dialogue with your partner and role-play it. The following references may be of some help.

Reference:

personal leave; sick leave; annual leave; official leave; marriage leave; funeral leave

take a leave/take a day off

take a 3-day leave/take 3 days off

ask for leave

grant leave

Situation 2: Suppose you are on a business trip and you would like to talk with Anny, the receptionist, about the reservation. Make a dialogue with your partner and role-play it. The following references may be of *some help.*

Reference:

reservation; confirm; payment

check in; check out; wake up call

Welcome to our hotel, sir!

Would you please complete this registration form?

Could you sign your name, please?

Here is your key. Hope you enjoy your stay in our hotel.

A porter will take your luggage to your room.

Room service is available 24 hours a day.

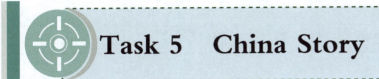

Task 5 China Story

New Words

crack	n.	裂缝
disciple	n.	弟子；门生
gravely	adv.	严肃地
sacrifice	v.	祭献
approach	v.	接近
rugged	adj.	崎岖的
pant	v.	喘气
earnest	adj.	真诚的
rebuff	n.	拒绝
surrender	v.	投降；放弃
grandiose	adj.	壮丽的
swirl	v.	旋转
crag	n.	悬崖
encompass	v.	包括；包围
panorama	n.	全景

Proper Names

Five Sacred Mountains 中国五岳
One Heaven Gate 一天门

Directions: Read the story and try to retell it.

任务内容	孔子登泰山的故事
任务目的	用英语传播中国儒家文化
任务形式	英语复述、角色扮演
职场技能	语言描述能力

Confucius Climbed Mount Tai

Early one morning, just at the **crack** of dawn, Confucius was about to leave his house, holding a walking stick and carrying a simple lunch. One of his **disciples** asked him, "Master, where are you going?" Confucius replied, cheerfully, "I'm going to climb Mount Tai."

His disciple was puzzled, "But Mount Tai is so high! If you, sir, an old man, wish to enjoy the scenery, why don't you climb a small mountain?"

Confucius replied **gravely**, "I'm not going to Mount Tai for pleasure. Mount Tai is regarded as the holiest of the **Five Sacred Mountains**; I'm going to pay my respects to Mount Tai and to investigate how the ancient rulers **sacrificed** on this mountain."

The disciple then said, "In that case, sir, let's go together."

They **approached** Mount Tai from the eastern road. Passing the **One Heaven Gate**, they turned north. The path grew progressively more **rugged**, and Confucius' steps became slower and he began to **pant** for breath. Every step seemed to get harder for him to make. His disciple said, "Master, let me help you." But the other replied, "There is no need. I can keep going."

His disciple then suggested, "Well, have a rest, sir. Besides, we don't have to go right to the top."

Confucius looked back down at the way they had come, and said in an **earnest** tone, "This path is like the road of life—full of thorns and briars. I have visited a number of states, and everywhere met with **rebuffs**. But I never thought of abandoning my quest or **surrendering**. We must go right to the top!"

The disciple raised no more objections, and the pair eventually reached the summit.

Standing on the topmost peak and gazing down at the **grandiose** scenery amid the **swirling** "sea of clouds", with **crag** after crag stretching into the distance, Confucius said with deep emotion, "By climbing Mount Tai, one can **encompass** the whole world at a single glance. Suddenly all the sufferings and hardships of humanity become of no consequence. By standing on a high place you get a broad **panorama** of things, and that way your horizons become wider. This mountain really is a place to offer sacrifices!"

His disciple said, "Now I understand, Master, that Mount Tai is a symbol of nobility."

Confucius nodded in satisfaction.

(390 words)

Checklist

1=Least Confident   2=Somewhat Confident   3=Extremely Confident

Learning Outcome Checklist	1	2	3
I am familiar with strong and weak reading.			
I get familiar with rhyme.			
I can talk about my workplace routine.			
The language of my presentation is correct and clear.			
I can retell the Chinese story *Confucius Climbed Mount Tai*.			

2

Unit 2

Working Environment

Learning Focus

单元内容	Enjoying English	1）缩读 2）缩读 3）名言与绕口令 4）歌曲：*Yesterday Once More* 昨日重现
	Testing Your Ears	1）环境条例 2）未来的汽车 3）技术时代
	Talking Together	1）科技的两面性 2）经济发展趋势
	Training Task	1）未来科技 2）环境
	China Story	*Quantum Communication* 量子通信
单元目标	语言知识目标	能够用英语描述职场环境
	语言技能目标	1）能够听懂职场环境相关的对话 2）能够用英语谈论职场环境
	学习策略	努力营造沉浸式的英语学习氛围，创造英语学习环境
	情感态度	初步形成人与自然和谐相处的意识
	文化意识	讲中国故事，关注中国科技发展，增强民族自豪感
	职业素养	培养与时俱进的科技创新精神

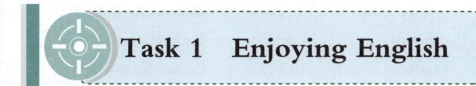

Task 1　Enjoying English

Part 1

English Abbreviations　(1)

任务内容	辨析缩读
任务目的	能够在口语中运用缩读
任务形式	听，跟读
训练技能	地道的缩读技巧

Directions: *Listen and repeat.*

and	→ You'n me.
are	→ They're gone.
are you	→ Where ya going?
because	→ No, 'cause I don't like it.
could have	→ could'a
	→ He could'a finished it if...
could not have	→ couldn'a
	→ He couldn'a done it.
did you	→ didja or 'dja
	→ How didja go there?
	or How 'dja go there?
do you	→ 'dy'a

	→ How 'dy'a do?	
don't know	→ dunno	→ I dunno.
give me	→ gimme	→ Gimme that book.
going to	→ gonna	→ I'm gonna see a doctor.
Goodbye	→ g'bye	→ I'm leaving now. G'bye.
got to	→ gotta	→ I gotta see him.
him	→ 'im	→ Tell 'im so.
let me	→ lem'me	→ lem'me go.
of	→ a	→ I sorta like him.
	→ o'	→ It's made o' wood.
old	→ ol'	→ It's an ol' man.
out of	→ outta	→ Get outta here!
sure	→ sher	→ Are you sher?

Part 2

English Abbreviations (2)

任务内容	辨析缩读
任务目的	能够在口语中运用缩读
任务形式	听，跟读
训练技能	地道的缩读技巧

Directions: Listen and repeat.

want to	→ wanna	→ I wanna go.
What are you	→ wachya	→ Wachya doing?
	→ wacha	→ Wacha doing?
What did you	→ wudidya	→ Wudidya buy?
	→ wudjya	→ Wudjya buy?

	→ wudja	→ Wudja buy?
What do you	→ wuddy'a	→ Wuddy'a want?
What is the	→ what'sa	→ What'sa matter?
Why did you	→ whyd'ya	→ Whyd'ya go?
	→ whydja	→ Whydja go?
Why do you	→ why'dy'a	→ Why'dy'a work so hard?
you	→ ya	→ How are ya?
	→ y'	→ Did y' ever see him?

Part 3

Proverbs and Tongue Twisters

（1）Proverbs

任务内容	学习名言警句
任务目的	从名言中获得启迪
任务形式	熟读，背诵
训练技能	启智增慧

Directions: Read the following proverbs after the recording and practice more by yourself.

Walls have ears.

隔墙有耳。

A man without knowledge is like a house without a foundation.

人无知如房无基。

Don't put off till tomorrow what should be done today.

今日事，今日毕。

Storms make trees take deeper roots.

风暴使树木深深扎根。

Shallow streams make most din; still waters run deep.
溪浅声喧,静水流深。

(2) Tongue Twisters

任务内容	练习绕口令
任务目的	提升口语流利度
任务形式	自主练习,小组竞赛
训练技能	听音、辨音和发音能力

Directions: Read the following tongue twisters after the recording and practice more by yourself.

A cheeky chimp chucked cheap chocolate chips in the cheap chocolate chip shop.
一只厚脸皮的黑猩猩把便宜的巧克力片扔进了便宜的巧克力薯条店。

The drummers drummed and the strummers strummed.
鼓手们敲打着,弹奏手们弹拨着。

James jostled Jean while Jean jostled Joan.
詹姆斯推挤珍,珍推挤琼。

Some slow sloths sleep soundly.
慢吞吞的树懒睡得很香。

Drew dripped the drink from the dipper, but he did not drink a drop.
饮料从勺子里滴落下来,但德鲁一滴也没喝。

Enjoy Yourself

Directions: Listen to the song and sing along.

Yesterday Once More 昨日重现

When I was young

当我年轻时

I'd listen to the radio

常听收音机

Waiting for my favorite songs

等待心爱的歌曲

When they played I'd sing along

听到播放时便随声歌唱

It made me smile

这使我欢畅

Those were such happy times

那是多么幸福的时刻

And not so long ago

就在不久前

How I wondered where they'd gone

我想知道他们曾去何处

But they're back again

但是他们又回来了

Just like a long-lost friend

像一位久未谋面的朋友

All the songs I loved so well

那些歌我依旧喜欢

Every Sha-la-la-la

每一声 Sha-la-la-la

Every Wo-o-wo-o

每一声 Wo-o-wo-o

Still shines

仍然闪亮

Every shing-a-ling-a-ling

每一声 shing-a-ling-a-ling

Notes

That they're starting to sing

当他们开始唱时

So fine

如此欢畅

When they get to the part

当他们唱到一个地方

Where he's breaking her heart

令她伤心断肠

It can really make me cry

这真能叫我哭出来

Just like before

一如往昔

It's yesterday once more

仿佛昔日又重来

(Shoobie do lang lang)

（无比惆怅）

(Shoobie do lang lang)

（无比惆怅）

Looking back on how it was in years gone by

回首过去的几年

And the good times that I had

我曾有过的欢乐时光

Makes today seem rather sad

使今天显得更加悲伤

So much has changed

变化多大啊

It was songs of love that I would sing to them

这就是那些跟着唱过的旧情歌

And I memorize each word

我会记住每一个字眼

Those old melodies

那些古老旋律

Still sound so good to me

在我听来仍然那么动听

As they melt the years away

好像他们把岁月融消

Every Sha-la-la-la

每一声 Sha-la-la-la

Every Wo-o-wo-o

每一声 Wo-o-wo-o

Still shines

仍然闪亮

Every shing-a-ling-a-ling

每一声 shing-a-ling-a-ling

That they're starting to sing

当他们开始唱时

So fine

如此欢畅

All my best memories

我所有的美好回忆

Come back clearly to me

清晰地重现

Some can even make me cry

有一些仍能使我哭出来

Just like before

一如往昔

It's yesterday once more

仿佛昔日又重来

Every Sha-la-la-la

每一声 Sha-la-la-la

Every Wo-o-wo-o

每一声 Wo-o-wo-o

Still shines

仍然闪亮

Every shing-a-ling-a-ling

每一声 shing-a-ling-a-ling

That they're starting to sing

当他们开始唱时

So fine

如此欢畅

Every Sha-la-la-la

每一声 Sha-la-la-la

Every Wo-o-wo-o

每一声 Wo-o-wo-o

Still shines

仍然闪亮

Task 2 Testing Your Ears

New Words

expansion	n.	扩大,膨胀,扩充
vanish	v.	消失
habitat	n.	（动植物的）产地,栖息地
indigenous	adj.	土生土长的
species	n.	（单复同）物种,种类
aerodynamics	n.	空气动力学
diesel	n.	柴油
standpoint	n.	立场,观点
cookie	n.	网络饼干
browser	n.	浏览器
format	n.	格式

Proper Names

the Commodity Inspection Bureau 商检局

Part 1

Environmental Regulations

任务内容	关于环境条例的对话
任务目的	学会用英语谈论企业发展与环境之间的关系
任务形式	听，填词
职场技能	合理解决企业的发展与环境保护的关系

Directions: *Listen to the following dialogue twice and fill in the blanks.*

A: What's holding us back on the plant expansion (1)_____? We were supposed to see the specs on that ages ago. Why haven't I heard anything about it? Did the whole project just vanish into thin air?

B: No, sir. The plant expansion project has been delayed. There was a snag up in the filing process to get the necessary (2)_____ permits. It seems that the property we were slated to build on is also habitat for some endangered indigenous species.

A: You're joking, right? No wonder we've been tied up with this project. I know the environmental (3)_____ statement will take forever to get (4)_____ if they've found anything endangered on the site. Are they positive there is (5)_____ of

endangered species actually living there?

B: The environmental review board has a team on it now. Hopefully we'll know more by the end of the week.

Cars of the Future

任务内容	关于未来汽车的对话
任务目的	学会用英语谈论未来汽车新科技
任务形式	听，填短语
职场技能	关注行业科技发展前沿

Directions: *Listen to the following dialogue twice and fill in the blanks.*

A: Now, Phil, you mentioned that you actually studied automotive engineering.

B: Yeah, that's correct.

A: OK, can you explain what automotive engineering is?

B: It's basically car design and basically technology (1)_____ _____cars (2)_____: the engine, the performance, the aerodynamics, so it's basically an overview of all kinds of car aspects for the future.

A: Cool, so you must know a lot about the cars of the future and stuff. I mean, how do you see cars in, let's say, twenty years, thirty years, forty years?

B: (3)_____, I think the big developments will be alternative fuels. (4)_____, petrol and diesel engines are causing a lot of damage to the planet and we're going to eventually (5) _____ natural resources, so I think the developments will be towards electric or hybrid cars.

A: Right.

B: Maybe even using fuel cells such as hydrogen.

A: Well, like how many years away do you think this is?

B: Realistically, ten to fifteen years away before we start seeing the first ones in production. But before we see everyone using them, it's going to be twenty years. I would have thought. I guess.

Part 3

Web-based Marketing

任务内容	关于网络营销的对话
任务目的	学会用英语讨论网络营销
任务形式	听，填句子
职场技能	能够利用网络促进企业营销

Directions: Listen to the following dialogue twice and fill in the blanks.

A: (1) _____? How effective do you think it is from a marketing standpoint?

B: We've been able to survey and track some of the information of our website users through some cookie technology, and (2) _____.

A: What kinds of hits are we getting on our company's website?

B: From the numbers, it seems nearly half of the visitors who stumble onto our page pick up the link not from network browsers or search engines, but from our circular insert. That means our consumers are purposefully and actively seeking information about our products and services through the web format. Based on these findings, I am completely convinced (3)_____.

A: You really think that many people turn to the Internet to find product information. What about the old standbys of word mouth and print media?

B: Well, (4)_____. They aren't a thing of the past. But I think they might be less important now than in the past. (5)_____!

Task 3　Talking Together

New Words

clutter	v.	使……凌乱
versus	prep.	与……相对
deficit	n.	赤字,逆差
recession	n.	经济衰退
stagnant	adj.	停滞的,不景气的
outsource	v.	外包
inflation	n.	通货膨胀

Duality of Science and Technology

任务内容	关于科技两面性的对话
任务目的	用英语谈论科技的两面性
任务形式	朗读对话，角色扮演
职场技能	辩证地认识与利用新科技

Conversation 1:

Directions: Complete the following dialogue according to the hints given in Chinese and role-play it with your partner.

A: So, Jeff, let's talk about technology. These days we have (1)_____ _____ (各种各样的) new technology, computers, ...

B: Can we just end this right now? I don't like technology, so can we talk about something else?

A: What? You don't like technology?

B: No, I don't like technology.

A: What do you mean you don't like technology?

B: Technology is... I think it's (2)_____ (与……背道而驰) what it was originally invented for, and that is for convenience to make people's lives more easy and to give them more (3)_____ ____ (自由时间).

A: Yeah, but technology does make your life easier, like it (4)_____ _____ us _____ (节省时间), it communicates, ...

B: But does it save us time?

A: I think so. I mean, now the phone is in your pocket. You can just pick it up and call anytime, anywhere in the world.

B: Kind of. I kind of agree with that, but sometimes that walk to the phone is sort of pleasant and you had time to think about other things. But now as you're on the phone, you get into your car and you drive to your office and the first thing you do is to check your e-mail and then right after that you check your voice mail and then you send an e-mail to someone and then..., I think it's just sort of—it's cluttered. It's cluttered our life versus cleaning it up.

A: Yeah, but maybe if you did not have that, then you would probably have something else that would just clutter up your life. I'm sure people were busy before they had technology.

B: Mm, I agree. I think they were busy with more wholesome things. I don't think we have to see so much news or read so

Notes

many different things（5）_____（在网上）. When was the last time you wrote a letter, a nice hand-written letter, to one of your friends, put it in an envelope and put it in the mailbox?

A: About three or four years.

B: Or a postcard even?

A: Four years.

B: So, I think technology is good but it sometimes defeats its own original purpose.

Part 2

Economy Development Trend

任务内容	关于经济发展趋势对话
任务目的	用英语谈论经济发展趋势
任务形式	朗读对话，角色扮演
职场技能	关注经济发展

Conversation 2:

Directions: *Place the following sentences in correct order to form a dialogue and role-play it with your partner.*

a. Increasing exports would weaken the currency.

b. What worries me the most is the trade deficit.

c. I really think we're headed for a recession.

d. If unemployment falls, there's pressure to increase pay.

e. If more people are working, it will give the economy a boost.

A: It's hard to be optimistic about things with the way the economy's headed...The trade deficit is getting larger. Consumption's down...
（1）_____

B: The economy has been stagnant for a while now. We've been in a recessive state for several months already. (2)_____ I think the government should do more to encourage exports.

A: (3)_____ I think the main point is economic growth. We need more jobs. Factories have outsourced and moved many jobs to foreign countries. The result is an increase in unemployment in our own country, lower consumption, lower production, and an overall feeble economy. (4)_____

B: It's true that we should do something about unemployment, but what about inflation? (5)_____ That would result in inflation, which would result in a much less dynamic economy.

Notes

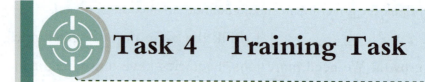

Task 4　Training Task

任务内容	1）未来科技 2）环境
任务目的	能用英语完成未来科技与环境的讨论
任务形式	角色扮演
职场技能	关注行业科技发展以及环境保护

Directions: Make dialogues for the following situations. You can refer to the words, expressions and patterns given below.

Situation 1: *Two students are talking about the technology in the future. Please make up a dialogue and act it out with your partners.*

Reference:

scientific achievement; scientific instrument;

artificial intelligence; space exploration/space research;

mechanical labor; household appliance;

promote the development of human society;

We've been able to survey and track...

Based on these findings, ...

I think the big developments will be...

Situation 2: *Two students are discussing the relationship between the technological development and the environment. Please make up a dialogue and act it out with your partners.*

Reference:

renewable energy sources; depletion of resources;

energy crisis; set foot on; endangered species;

environment deterioration; global warming;

life expectancy/life span;

be on the verge of extinction; hostile environment;

advantage; counterbalance

Task 5 China Story

New Words

quantum	n.	量子
encrypt	v.	把……加密或编码
eavesdropper	n.	窃听者
intercept	v.	拦截,拦阻
academician	n.	院士
odor	n.	气味
unprecedented	adj.	空前的

Directions: Read the story and try to retell it.

任务内容	量子通信的介绍
任务目的	用英语描述中国新科技
任务形式	英语复述
职场技能	语言描述能力

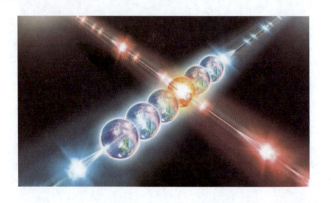

Quantum Communication

What is **quantum** communication? The scientific world defines it as a "method of communication using quantum effects on communications cycles". Simply put, it is a method of **encrypted** communication. This technology has grown organically from encrypted messaging, and is virtually unbreakable.

How are messages sent by quantum encryption safer? It is because particles of light cannot be divided. An **eavesdropper** cannot divide a particle of light into two parts, nor can a message in a particle of light be read by a third party or transmitted elsewhere. Such a message may be detected, but it cannot be understood. So quantum physics can protect such secret codes, as they can neither be **intercepted** nor cracked.

China has poured a huge amount of effort into research in this field, and has achieved results attracting world attention. Among these achievements is the immortal work of Academician Pan Jianwei, who has been called China's youngest **academician**.

The fruit of Academician Pan's scientific research into quantum communication was chosen as one of "Ten Worldwide Science and Technology Advances" in 1997. He was only twenty-seven years old at that time. At the age of thirty-one he abandoned the comfortable treatment he was being given abroad, and determinedly returned to his native land to set up his own laboratory and devote himself heart and soul to research. To doubters he would say, "I seek neither fame nor profit. I have only one aim—to repay my native land, which gave me birth and raised me. I want to make my country stronger!" His research put China in the leading place in the world in quantum communication. Pan and his work have been evaluated as follows: "He has a child-like form of curiosity about the world, wishing to sniff the **odor** of each fallen leaf, and combines this with science. He stands in the front rank of the world, holds dialogs with the universe, has the reputation of a sage, and has made an **unprecedented** achievement."

（346 words）

Checklist

1=Least Confident 2=Somewhat Confident 3=Extremely Confident

Learning Outcome Checklist	1	2	3
I am familiar with English abbreviations.			
I get familiar with some new technologies.			
I can talk about the working environment.			
The language of my presentation is correct and clear.			
I can give a brief introduction to the Chinese story *Quantum Communication*.			

Unit 3
Output Quality

Learning Focus

单元内容	Enjoying English	1）单词重音及短语中的重读词 2）句中的重读词 3）名言与绕口令 4）歌曲：*Be What You Wanna Be* 成为你想成为的人
	Testing Your Ears	1）产品质量 2）产品介绍 3）索赔与理赔
	Talking Together	1）退货 2）投诉
	Training Task	1）产品质量 2）处理投诉
	China Story	*Zhaozhou Bridge* 赵州桥
单元目标	语言知识目标	能够用英语描述产品质量并处理投诉与理赔
	语言技能目标	1）能够听懂与产品质量、投诉与理赔相关的对话 2）能够用英语谈论产品质量和处理投诉与理赔
	学习策略	学会记笔记，把握要点
	情感态度	培养热情、真诚、礼貌的服务态度
	文化意识	讲中国故事，感悟劳动人民的智慧和才干，增强民族自豪感
	职业素养	培养良好的人际沟通能力，能恰当地处理客户的索赔与投诉

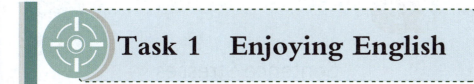

Task 1　Enjoying English

Stresses in Words or Phrases

任务内容	辨析单词重音及短语中的重读词
任务目的	把握单词正确发音，体会不同重读对语义的影响
任务形式	听，回答，跟读
训练技能	提升多元文化交流能力

Directions: You will hear eight sentences. After each sentence, there will be a pause of ten seconds. During the pause, circle the word or phrase with the correct stress as you hear in each sentence. The sentences will be spoken only once.

1. My little brother really likes the **'dessert/ des'sert**.
2. My friend has a **'hot dog/ hot 'dog**.
3. Please turn to page **'fifty/ fif 'teen**.
4. Can you see a **black 'board/ 'blackboard** in the classroom?
5. Have you ever seen a **'yellow jacket/ yellow 'jacket**?
6. The students met their **'English teacher/ English 'teacher** on the street.
7. She lives in the **White 'House/ 'White House**.
8. He will be **'eighty/ eigh'teen** next year.

Notes

Part 2

Sentence Stresses

任务内容	辨析句中的重读词
任务目的	体会不同重读对语义的影响
任务形式	听，辨析，讨论
训练技能	恰当运用重读词表情达意，顺畅交流

Directions: *You will hear eight sentences. After each sentence, there will be a pause of ten seconds. During the pause, circle the letter in front of the sentence which has the right stressed word according to what you hear. The sentences will be spoken only once.*

1. a. There are THREE cats in the street.

    b. There are three CATS in the street.

2. a. Jane told me that the DOG was under the table.

    b. Jane told me that the dog was under the TABLE.

3. a. Do you go to SCHOOL by bike?

    b. Do you go to school by BIKE?

4. a. The SHOP has a beautiful environment around it.

    b. The shop has a BEAUTIFUL environment around it.

5. a. I gave HIM a book yesterday.

    b. I gave him a BOOK yesterday.

6. a. I like chocolate ICE CREAM.

    b. I like CHOCOLATE ice cream.

7. a. He called Mrs. Green to tell her that he would arrive a little LATER than 6 o'clock.

b. He called MRS. GREEN to tell her that he would arrive a little later than 6 o'clock.

8. a. The GIRL was so surprised to hear the result.

b. The girl was so SURPRISED to hear the result.

Proverbs and Tongue Twisters

（1）Proverbs

任务内容	学习名言警句
任务目的	从名言中获得启迪
任务形式	熟读，背诵
训练技能	启智增慧

Directions: *Read the following proverbs after the recording and practice more by yourself.*

Jack of all trades, master of none.

样样皆通，样样稀松。

Look before you leap.

三思而后行。

Let bygones be bygones.

过去的就让它过去吧。

It's hard to please all.

众口难调。

When in Rome, do as the Romans do.

入乡随俗。

（2）Tongue Twister

任务内容	练习绕口令
任务目的	提升口语流利度
任务形式	自主练习，小组竞赛
训练技能	听音、辨音和发音能力

Directions: Read the following tongue twister after the recording and practice more by yourself.

She sells seashells on the seashore,
她在海滩上卖海贝壳，

The shells she sells are seashells, I'm sure.
我确信她卖的贝壳是真的海贝壳。

For if she sells seashells on the seashore,
因为如果她在海滩上卖海贝壳，

Then I'm sure she sells seashore shells.
我确信她卖的是海滩贝壳。

Part 4

Enjoy Yourself

Directions: Listen to the song and sing along.

Be What You Wanna Be 成为你想成为的人

Doctor, actor, lawyer or a singer
医生、演员、律师或歌唱家

Why not president
为什么不是总统

Be a dreamer
做一个有梦想的人

You can be just the one you wanna be
你可以成为任何一个你想成为的人
Policeman, fire fighter or a post man
警察、消防员或者邮递员
Why not something like your old man
为什么不是像你老爸一样呢
You can be just the one you wanna be
你可以成为任何一个你想成为的人
Doctor, actor, lawyer or a singer
医生、演员、律师或者歌唱家
Why not president
为什么不是总统
Be a dreamer
做一个有梦想的人
You can be just the one you wanna be
你可以成为任何一个你想成为的人
I know that we all got one thing
我知道我们都得到一样东西
That we all share together
那就是我们都在分享的
We got that one nice dream
我们都拥有一个美好的梦想
We live for
我们为之生存
You never know what life could bring
你不会知道生活会给你带来什么
'cause nothing last forever
因为没有什么能永恒
Just hold on to the team you play for

为了你所努力的团队坚持住

I know you could reach the top
我知道你会达到顶峰

Make sure that you won't stop
你一定不要停下来

Be the one that you wanna be
做那个你一直都想成为的人

Now sing this with me
现在和我一起歌唱

Doctor, actor, lawyer or a singer
医生、演员、律师或歌唱家

Why not president
为什么不是总统

Be a dreamer
做一个有梦想的人

You can be just the one you wanna be
你可以成为任何一个你想成为的人

Policeman, fire fighter or a post man
警察、消防员或者邮递员

Why not something like your old man
为什么不是像你老爸一样呢

You can be just the one you wanna be
你可以成为任何一个你想成为的人

We may have different ways to think
我们也许会从不同角度考虑问题

But it doesn't really matter
但这没关系

We all caught up in the steam of this life
我们都赶上了这次人生之旅

Focus on every little thing
执着于每一件琐事

That's what does really matter
这才是问题所在

Luxury cars and bling
豪车和珠宝

That's not real life
那都不是真正的生活

I know you could reach the top
我知道你会达到顶峰

Make sure that you won't stop
确定你不会停下来

Be the one that you wanna be
做那个你一直都想成为的人

Now sing this with me
现在和我一起歌唱

Doctor, actor, lawyer or a singer
医生、演员、律师或歌唱家

Why not president,
为什么不是总统

Be a dreamer
做一个有梦想的人

You can be just the one you wanna be
你可以成为任何一个你想成为的人

Policeman, fire fighter or a post man
警察、消防员或者邮递员

Why not something like your old man
为什么不是像你老爸一样呢

You can be just the one you wanna be

你可以成为任何一个你想成为的人

Last year I used to dream about this day

去年我还在梦想着有这么一天

Now I'm here

现在这一切都实现了

I'm singing for you

我将为你而唱

I hope I could inspire you

我希望我能鼓舞你的斗气

'cause I've got all the love, 'cause I've got all love for you

因为我得到了所有的爱，所有想给予你的爱

Doctor, actor, lawyer or a singer

医生、演员、律师或歌唱家

Why not president

为什么不是总统

Be a dreamer

做一个有梦想的人

You can be just the one you wanna be

你可以成为任何一个你想成为的人

Policeman, fire fighter or a post man

警察、消防员或者邮递员

Why not something like your old man

为什么不是像你老爸一样呢

You can be just the one you wanna be

你可以成为任何一个你想成为的人

Doctor, actor, lawyer or a singer

医生、演员、律师或歌唱家

Why not president,

为什么不是总统

Be a dreamer
做一个有梦想的人

You can be just the one you wanna be
你可以成为任何一个你想成为的人

Policeman, fire fighter or a post man
警察、消防员或者邮递员

Why not something like your old man
为什么不是像你老爸一样呢

You can be just the one you wanna be
你可以成为任何一个你想成为的人

Doctor, actor, lawyer or a singer
医生、演员、律师或歌唱家

Why not president
为什么不是总统

Be a dreamer
做一个有梦想的人

You can be just the one you wanna be
你可以成为任何一个你想成为的人

Policeman, fire fighter or a post man
警察、消防员或者邮递员

Why not something like your old man
为什么不是像你老爸一样呢

You can be just the one you wanna be
你可以成为任何一个你想成为的人

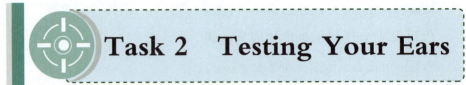

Task 2　Testing Your Ears

New Words

certificate	n.	证明书
rusty	adj.	生锈的
stain	n.	污点,污渍
dampness	n.	潮湿
stipulate	v.	规定,明确要求
plus	n.	优势,好处
compact	adj.	紧凑的,小型的
bale	n.	包,大捆
salvage	v.	挽救,挽回
compromise	v.	妥协,折中
preferential	adj.	优惠的

Part 1

Product Quality

任务内容	关于产品质量的对话
任务目的	学会用英语沟通产品质量问题
任务形式	听,填词
职场技能	能够有效沟通产品质量问题

Directions: *Listen to the following dialogue twice and fill in the blanks.*

A: We'd like to have you help straighten out the (1)_____ concerning the bicycles.

B: OK, can you give me the facts?

A: We have here a copy of the inspection certificate issued by the Commodity Inspection Bureau and a set of photos. The inspection certificate states that the bikes were found rusty when they were unpacked and the photos taken on the spot back up the (2)_____.

B: Are all our bikes like this?

A: Not all, there are 5 of them that have rust stains.

B: That is very (3)_____. Our manufacturer has always attached great importance to the quality of their products. But maybe the rust stains are due to dampness at the sea. If that's the case, the liability should rest with the insurance people.

A: But our experts are of the opinion that the rust stains are not due to dampness but due to poor workmanship. Please look at the picture. They surely (4)_____ that the derusting of the bikes before plating was not thoroughly done.

B: Well, it seems that manufacturers have not lived up to their (5)_____ in this case.

A: On the strength of this evidence, the responsibility rest with the producer and not with the insurance people. It's obvious that the manufacturers didn't strictly observe the proceeding requirements as stipulated in our contract.

B: Well, I'm very sorry for this. We'll replace the defective bikes with new ones.

A: Thank you for sorting out the matter for us.

Notes

Part 2

Product Introduction

任务内容	关于产品介绍的对话
任务目的	学会用英语推介产品
任务形式	听，填短语
职场技能	能够成功推介产品与服务

Directions: *Listen to the following dialogue twice and fill in the blanks.*

A: Could you give us a detailed description of the properties of your product?

B: OK. The X2500 has the unique feature of providing better data flow with less (1)_____. It will reduce your work load (2)_____.

A: Could you tell me more about it?

B: Of course. One of the real pluses of this product is that it is (3)_____, and of compact size. No one can match us (4)_____ as quality is concerned.

A: Can you introduce its (5)_____ to me?

B: We have this item in three price level.

A: We need the best possible quality.

B: That means this one.

A: I see, that's what I will order.

Claim and Compensation

任务内容	关于索赔与理赔的对话
任务目的	学会用英语进行索赔与理赔
任务形式	听，填句子
职场技能	能够有效处理客户的索赔与理赔

Directions: *Listen to the following dialogue twice and fill in the blanks.*

A: Have you checked how much of the contents of the damaged bales can still be used?

B: The report said that the majority could be salvaged. About 20% can't be used or sold out. (1)_____. We had counted on receiving the shipment to complete several orders.

A: (2)_____.

B: I'm sure we can count on your support to help us to overcome the present difficulty.

A: (3)_____?

B: We are willing to accept the shipment if you will allow a 30% reduction in price.

A: Let's compromise on a 20% reduction in price on this shipment. And for your next order, we'll give you some preferential terms in addition to what you are getting from us now.

B: (4)_____. We accept the proposal.
   (5)_____.

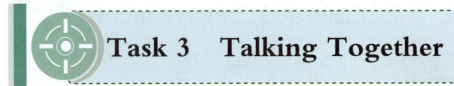

Task 3　Talking Together

New Words

paintwork	n.	漆面, 油漆层
spray	v.	喷, 喷洒
postage	n.	邮费, 邮资
express	adj.	特快的
refund	n.	退款

Part 1

Return of Goods

任务内容	关于退货的对话
任务目的	学会用英语处理退货
任务形式	角色扮演
职场技能	能够妥善处理退货

Conversation 1:

Directions: *Complete the following dialogue according to the hints given in Chinese and role-play it with your partner.*

A: The paintwork on the body of the cars has become discolored.

B: We have looked into the matter and found it was（1）_____

_____（由于）a chemical imbalance in the paint used in spraying the vehicles.

A: I'll return the goods to you, postage and packing forward.

B:（2）_____（事实上）we are taking these models out of production and calling in all those that we have supplied.

A: That's fine. When do you think we can get the replacements?

B: We have（3）_____（联系）our own suppliers and they said the replacements are on their way to us by express train. You should receive them within a week.

A: This is our initial order with which you and we are far from satisfied.

B: I（4）_____（道歉）for the inconvenience and please permit me to point out that this kind of fault rarely occurs in our factory. This is the first time, and I（5）_____（承诺）, it'll also be the last time. Please trust me.

Part 2

Complaining

任务内容	关于投诉的对话
任务目的	学会用英语处理投诉
任务形式	角色扮演
职场技能	掌握处理客户投诉的能力和技能

Conversation 2:

Directions: Place the following sentences in correct order to form a dialogue and role-play it with your partner.

a. I will give you a partial refund for the unsatisfactory tour.

b. I want a full refund.

c. Please tell me what went wrong.

d. Well, that's out of our control.

e. I'm sorry you have a complaint.

A: I want to make a complaint about the all-day bus tour I took yesterday.

B: (1)_____

A: I actually have a few complaints.

B: (2)_____

A: We were stuck in traffic for an hour.

B: (3)_____

A: The bus had no air conditioning.

B: It was 60 degrees out yesterday though.

A: (4)_____

B: I can't give you a full refund since you enjoyed part of the tour.

A: How about a partial refund then?

B: (5)_____

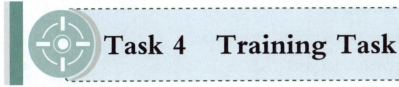

Task 4　Training Task

任务内容	1）产品质量 2）投诉处理
任务目的	能用英语进行产品介绍，处理投诉和理赔
任务形式	角色扮演
职场技能	产品介绍与投诉、理赔沟通能力

Directions: Make dialogues for the following situations. You can refer to the words, expressions and patterns given below.

Situation 1: A salesman and a customer are discussing about the quality of the printer. Please make up a dialogue and act it out with your partners.

Reference:

I'm sorry to hear that. Can you tell me what the issue is?

We apologize for the inconvenience.

Ok, I can arrange that for you. Is there anything else I can do for you?

If the quality of your initial shipment is found satisfactory, large repeats will follow.

We sincerely hope the quality is in conformity with the contract stipulations.

As long as the quality is good, it hardly matters if the price is a little bit higher.

We always have faith in the quality of your products.

Situation 2: The shipment of the air-conditioners were delayed.

The customer and the salesman are talking about it on the phone. Please make up a dialogue and act it out it with your partners.

Reference:

The hot season is rapidly approaching.

What can I do for you?

We hope you will send ... as soon as possible.

The goods we ordered are seasonal goods. So it will be better to ship them all at once.

In order to be in time for the season, early shipment is of utmost importance to us.

If shipment is too late, we will be forced to withdraw the contract.

Maybe next month is OK.

But we have informed you 3 times.

If you still delay delivery, I'll have to cancel the order.

Task 5　China Story

New Words

supervise	v.	监督，管理
craftsman	n.	工匠，手艺人
original	adj.	独创的，新颖的
span	n.	（桥或拱的）墩距；跨距
spandrel	n.	连梁；拱肩
parallel	adj.	平行的，极相似的
overflow	v.	溢出，漫出
immortal	n.	神
hoof	n.	蹄
rut	n.	车辙

Directions: *Read the story and try to retell it.*

任务内容	赵州桥的故事
任务目的	用英语介绍中国建筑
任务形式	英语复述
职场技能	语言描述能力

Zhaozhou Bridge

Zhaozhou Bridge is also called Anji Bridge. It is on the Jiaohe

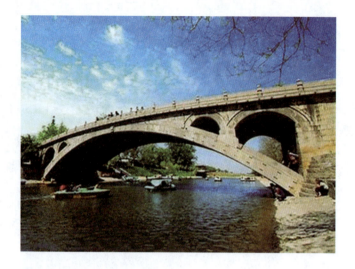

River to the south of Zhaoxian County town, 45 kilometers southeast of Shijiazhuang, Hebei Province. Because the whole bridge was made of stone materials, it was called Big Stone Bridge by the local people. It was first built between 595-605 and the construction was **supervised** by Li Chun, a famous **craftsman** in the Sui Dynasty.

The structure of Zhaozhou Bridge is **original**, and the appearance is beautiful. The bridge is 64.4 meters long, 9.6 meters wide and the **span** is 37.2 meters. It is a single-hole arc bridge made up of 28 comparatively separate arches. The greatest scientific contribution of Zhaozhou Bridge is its pioneering work of "open **spandrel**". At each shoulder of the main arch, there are 2 small **parallel** arches. This not only increases passages for the running water, decreases the weight of the bridge, and saves stone materials, but also enhances the stability of the bridge. Therefore, though 1,400 years has passed, having undergone many floods, eight earthquakes, and heavy traffic, it is still standing firm over the Jiaohe River.

There are many beautiful legends about the construction of Zhaozhou Bridge. In the past, the Jiaohe River **overflowed**, and the local people could only cross by boat. Lu Ban, the carpenters' ancestor, turned the sheep into stones overnight to make the bridge. Zhang

Guolao and Chai Wangye, two **immortals**, came to test the solidity of the bridge. Zhang Guolao rode on the donkey-back, facing backward. In the long bag on the donkey-back, there were the sun and the moon. Chai Wangye pushed a one-wheeled cart, on which there were the five famous mountains in China. When they came to the middle of the bridge, it began to shake and was likely to fall down. Seeing the situation was unfavorable, Lu Ban jumped into the water, and held up the bridge with his hands. Luckily, the bridge was safe and sound. So there left on the surface of the bridge clear **hoof** prints of the donkey and a **rut**. Lu Ban's fingerprints were also left on the arch of the bridge.

(365 words)

Checklist

1=Least Confident　　　2=Somewhat Confident　　　3=Extremely Confident

Learning Outcome Checklist	1	2	3
I am familiar with the stress.			
I get familiar with the product quality.			
I can make communication with the customers about the claim or compensation.			
The language of my presentation is correct and clear.			
I can retell the Chinese story *Zhaozhou Bridge*.			

Notes

Unit 4

Employment Security

Learning Focus

单元内容	Enjoying English	1）句子升降调 2）失去爆破 3）名言与绕口令 4）歌曲：*Carry on Till Tomorrow* 坚持到明天
	Testing Your Ears	1）规章制度 2）健康和安全保障 3）生产安全
	Talking Together	1）突发事件 2）网络安全
	Training Task	1）处理突发事件 2）应对网络安全
	China Story	*Search for Perfection* 零差错的"航空手艺人"
单元目标	语言知识目标	能够用英语描述职场安全
	语言技能目标	1）能够听懂与职场安全相关的对话 2）能够用英语谈论职场安全
	学习策略	迅速捕捉大意，创设情境，通过对话和反思进行合作学习
	情感态度	培养高度的安全意识和责任意识，提高防范能力
	文化意识	讲中国故事，传承工匠精神，增强民族自豪感
	职业素养	培养主人翁意识、爱岗敬业精神和敏捷的应变能力

Task 1　Enjoying English

Part 1

Rising-falling Intonation

任务内容	听录音，判断句子的语调
任务目的	学会使用不同语调表达特定情感
任务形式	听，回答
训练技能	语调的辨义能力

Directions: You will hear eight sentences. After each sentence, there will be a pause of ten seconds. During the pause, circle the letter next to the sentence you hear. The sentences will be spoken only once.

1. a. It's dark already. ↘

   b. It's dark already? ↗

2. a. Susan is in love with Sam. ↘

   b. Susan is in love with Sam? ↗

3. a. —I cannot do it by myself.

   　—What! ↘

   b. —I cannot do it by myself.

   　—What? ↗

4. a. Cindy can do it, can't she? ↘

   b. Cindy can do it, can't she? ↗

5. a. Should I use red ↗ or orange? ↘

b. Should I use red or orange? ↗

6. a. He is only a millionaire. ↘

   b. He is only a millionaire? ↗

7. a. The meeting is open today. ↘

   b. The meeting is open today? ↗

8. a. I can't eat anything. ↘

   b. I can't eat anything? ↗

Loss of Plosion

任务内容	听录音，找出句子中失去爆破的部分
任务目的	掌握失去爆破的发音技巧
任务形式	听，回答
训练技能	听音、辨音能力

Directions: You will hear some sentences. Repeat what you hear and underline the plosive consonants that undergo loss of plosion. Each sentence will be read twice.

1. I'm sure you also did a good job.

2. When will you start to work?

3. See you about four, then.

4. Did he help put out the fire?

5. This isn't the first time.

6. My girlfriend doesn't understand this play.

7. I don't think you can finish the paper.

8. Have you got lots of information about travel?

9. The old picture is great, too.

10. I'd like to say this is a good book.

Proverbs and Tongue Twisters

（1）Proverbs

任务内容	学习名言警句
任务目的	从名言中获得启迪
任务形式	熟读，背诵
训练技能	启智增慧

Directions: Read the following proverbs after the recording and practice more by yourself.

Pride goes before a fall.
骄者必败。

Lost time is never found again.
时间一去不再来。

He laughs best who laughs last.
谁笑在最后，谁笑得最好。

A little pot is soon hot.
量小易怒。

Speech is silver but silence is gold.
雄辩是银，沉默是金。

（2）Tongue Twister

任务内容	练习绕口令
任务目的	提升口语流利度
任务形式	自主练习，小组竞赛
训练技能	听音、辨音和发音能力

Directions: Read the following tongue twister after the recording and practice more by yourself.

Peter Pepper picked a pack of pickled pepper;
彼得·佩珀挑选了一包腌辣椒；
A pack of pickled pepper Peter Pepper picked;
一包彼得·佩珀挑选的腌辣椒；
If Peter Pepper picked a pack of pickled pepper,
如果彼得·佩珀拿了一包腌辣椒，
Where is the pack of pickled pepper Peter Pepper picked?
彼得·佩珀挑的那包腌辣椒在哪里？

Part 4

Enjoy Yourself

Directions: Listen to the song and sing along.

Carry on Till Tomorrow 坚持到明天

In younger days
在年轻的时候
I told myself my life would be my own
我告诉我自己世界是我的
And I'd leave the place where sunshine never shone
同时我离开了黑暗
For my life's too short for waiting
生命如此短暂，经不起等待
When I see the rising sun
当我看到太阳升起的时候
Then I know again that I must carry on
我知道我必须再一次继续前进
Carry on till tomorrow

一直坚持到明天

There's no reason to look back

没有任何理由去回头看

Carry on, carry on, carry on

向前，向前，向前

Beyond the shadows of the clouds

超过云的阴影

And onward to the sky

通向天空

Carry on till I find the rainbow's end

继续前进直到我找到彩虹的尽头

For my life's too short for waiting

生命如此短暂，经不起等待

When I see the rising sun

当我看到太阳升起的时候

Then I know again that I must carry on

我知道我必须再一次继续前进

Carry on till tomorrow

一直坚持到明天

There's no reason to look back

没有任何理由去回头看

Carry on, carry on, carry on

向前，向前，向前

Drifting on the wings of freedom

用自由的翅膀翱翔

Leave this stormy day

离开压抑的那些天

And we'll ride to tomorrow's golden fields

我们将骑向金色田野的明天

For my life's too short for waiting
生命如此短暂，经不起等待

When I see the rising sun
当我看到太阳升起的时候

Then I know again that I must carry on
我知道我必须再一次继续前进

Carry on, carry on, carry on
向前，向前，向前

And when the heavy journey's done
当沉重的旅行结束时

I'll rest my weary head
我会放松自己

For the world and its colors will be bright
世界将是多彩和明亮的

For my life's too short for waiting
生命如此短暂，经不起等待

When I see the rising sun
当我看到落日时

Then I know again that I must carry on
我知道我必须再一次继续前进

Carry on till tomorrow
一直坚持到明天

There's no reason to look back
没有任何理由去回头看

Carry on, carry on, carry on...
向前，向前，向前……

Task 2　Testing Your Ears

New Words

radioactive	adj.	放射性的
ear muffs	n.	耳套
draft	n.	草稿；草案
assessment	n.	评估
insurance	n.	保险
quote	n.	报价
premise	n.	前提
finalize	v.	把（计划、旅行、项目等）最后定下来
warehouse	n.	仓库

Office Rules

任务内容	关于规章制度的对话
任务目的	学会用英语讨论工作中的规章制度
任务形式	听，填词
职场技能	严格执行职业安全规范

Directions: Listen to the following dialogue twice and fill in the blanks.

A: Can I ask you what the office rules are?

B: Yes, do you know the nine to five (1)_____?

A: Is it from 9:00 to 12:00 in the morning and 1:00 to 5:00 in the afternoon?

B: Yes, you are right.

A: The (2)_____ in the lab is radioactive and dangerous, so work with (3)_____. Have you got ear muffs and gloves?

B: Do I have to (4)_____ ear muffs and gloves? I am not used to working with them on.

A: Yes, you have to. It is a (5)_____ rule of the company. You could not only lose your job but your hearing if you don't.

B: OK. I'll go and get a pair of them.

 Part 2

Health and Security

任务内容	关于职业健康和安全保障的对话
任务目的	学会用英语讨论职业健康和安全保障
任务形式	听，填短语
职场技能	注重职业健康和安全

Directions: Listen to the following dialogue twice and fill in the blanks.

A: As a reasonably large company, we are required to produce a written health and safety policy.

B: Have you got a draft copy for me to look at?

A: No, we are still doing the risk assessment of the main office building.

B: Well, this is a brand new office facility. It must be one of the safest place to work in the whole of Shanghai.

A: Yes, but you'd be surprised at all the ways that people can find to hurt themselves!

B: I know. So what about insurance? Where are we with that?

A: Well, our foreign employees will (1) _____ their own insurance.

B: And what about the Chinese employees?

A: We are going to have to (2) _____ company-wide cover for them. We are waiting for some quotes now.

B: Won't the insurance companies want to come and inspect the premises?

A: Yes, they will want to (3) _____ before finalizing any sort of cover.

B: We will just have to make sure that everything is completely satisfactory.

A: The building manager has been making all the preparations. There shouldn't be a problem.

B: OK. I'd better give him a call after this and make sure he has everything (4) _____.

A: The other thing I want to discuss is the first-aid programme we are planning to launch.

B: Sounds like a good idea! What do you have in mind?

A: The plan is to have at least one qualified first-aider on every floor in the office building.

B: So are we going to have to offer training if we don't have enough qualified people?

A: Yes, but it doesn't cost very much to (5) _____.

B: Great. Hopefully we'll get plenty of volunteers then.

Part 3

Production Safety

任务内容	关于生产安全的对话
任务目的	学会用英语讨论生产安全
任务形式	听，填句子
职场技能	主动发现、预警和防范能力

Directions: Listen to the following dialogue twice and fill in the blanks.

A: But, but...

B: Frankly, (1)_____. You're a hard worker but it doesn't mean you can go against company policy.

A: Oh, yes. Paul, (2)_____.

B: A misunderstanding? How can you explain the smell of cigarette smoke? (3)_____.

A: Let me explain. I went down to the warehouse to speak to Mr. Ingle and... well... someone else was smoking.

B: What? Someone was smoking in the warehouse? Golly gosh, (4)_____. Who was it, Anna?

A: Err... well... I can't really say. But I dealt with it and it won't happen again.

B: Thank you Anna and sorry about the misunderstanding. Would you like a biscuit? Now I really think (5)_____.

Task 3　Talking Together

New Words

evacuate	v.	撤离
panic	v.	惊慌
crash	v.	崩溃
antivirus	adj.	防病毒的

An Emergency

Conversation 1:

任务内容	关于突发事件的对话
任务目的	学会用英语描述突发事件
任务形式	角色扮演
职场技能	突发事件的快速应变能力

Directions: Complete the following dialogue according to the hints given in Chinese and role-play it with your partner.

A: What's (1) _____ (发生), officer?

B: There is a fire in your building. You need to evacuate immediately.

A: What? A fire? Oh, my God! What shall I do? Please get me out of here!

B: Don't panic! We'll help you get out of the building safely.

A: I can smell smoke!

B: Please（2）_____（听从我的指示）. Use a wet towel to（3）_____（遮住口鼻）. Walk quickly to the nearest emergency exit. Now go to get the wet towel.

A: OK.

B: Come with me.

A: Sir, I need to go back to get my jewelry box.

B: Don't take your（4）_____（私人物品）. We need to get out of the building now!

A: Gosh! I can see the flames!

B:（5）_____（蹲）and try not to breathe in the smoke.

Part 2

Network Security

任务内容	关于网络安全的对话
任务目的	学会用英语讨论网络安全防护
任务形式	角色扮演
职场技能	职场安全防护能力

Conversation 2:

Directions: Place the following sentences in correct order to form a dialogue and role-play it with your partner.

a. your computer can be easily infected by virus if you do that.

b. it was infected by a virus

c. And I take an antivirus software with me.
d. Is antivirus software necessary for a PC?
e. The system crashed

A: What can I do?
B: (1)_____ when I was surfing on the Internet.
A: Did you go to any illegal website?
B: No, but does that matter?
A: Yes, (2)_____
B: I see. I'd better never try.
A: That's wise.
B: Do you know what's wrong with my PC?
A: One minute. Oh, yes, (3)_____, and you had no antivirus software.
B: (4)_____
A: Of course. You'd better learn something about it.
B: I'm afraid yes. But what about the data I stored in the computer?
A: Don't worry. It should have been protected automatically. (5)_____ Do you want me to install it now?
B: Yes, please. I'll really appreciate that.

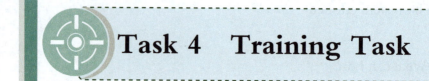

Task 4　Training Task

任务内容	1）处理突发事件 2）应对网络安全
任务目的	能够用英语描述突发事件与网络安全
任务形式	角色扮演
职场技能	培养安全意识与责任意识

Directions: Make dialogues for the following situations. You can refer to the words, expressions and patterns given below.

Situation 1: Suppose you are Li Lei from ABC Company, and you would like to talk with Peter, your partner, about the emergency. Make a dialogue with your partner and role-play it. The following references may be of some help.

Reference:

fire alarm; fire extinguisher; first-aid kit; safety inspection

Is the fire alarm working?

If you see a fire, raise the alarm.

Walk calmly to your nearest fire exit.

Meet at the fire assembly point.

Mind out. Don't get too close. It's very hot.

Mind you don't trip when you go past the packing area.

Situation 2: Suppose you are Li Lei from ABC Company, and you would like to talk with Peter, your partner, about network security. Make a dialogue with your partner and role-play it. The following references may be of some help.

Reference:

illegal; infect; virus; hackers

anti-virus software

There's something wrong with our computers.

We may never be able to trace the origin of this attack.

What we can do is work harder to make our systems impenetrable.

Many people almost never change their passwords.

I'm going to change my password right now!

A good password uses a mixture of letters and numbers.

Notes

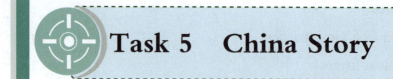

Task 5　China Story

New Words

routine	n.	常规
mumble	v.	咕哝
install	v.	安装
guarantee	v.	保证；保障
vibration	n.	振动；震动
conscientious	adj.	认真的
stride	n.	大步
agitation	n.	焦虑不安
craftsman	n.	工匠
substandard	adj.	不合格的

Proper Names

Shanghai Aircraft Manufacturing Co., Ltd. 上海飞机制造有限公司

Directions: Read the story and try to retell it.

任务内容	零差错的"航空手艺人"的故事
任务目的	传播工匠精神，激发创造活力，用英语讲述中国匠人故事
任务形式	英语复述
职场技能	语言描述能力

Search for Perfection

Late one night, Hu was lying exhausted on his bed. Although he was sleepy, he stuck to his nightly **routine**: to go over what he had done that day, including anything he may not have done well. He **mumbled** to himself, "This afternoon I tightened the screws on a large airplane I was going on, checked the safety catch, **installed** the external parts..."

Suddenly he sat upright on the bed, and slapped his head, "Did I check to see that everything was safe? I can't remember!"

"It won't be too late if you go and check tomorrow," his wife said, also sitting up. She poured a glass of water, and handed it to her husband.

"No, I must go and check right now; otherwise, I won't be able to sleep." He was adamant.

"But it's three o'clock in the morning," protested his wife, glancing at the bedside alarm clock with a pained expression.

Hu, already dressed, sat on the bed facing his wife. He explained, "It's vital that the screws be **guaranteed** to be properly tight to make sure that **vibrations** when the plane is in the air don't shake them loose. The lives of many people depend on even one tiny part. I dare not be the slightest bit careless! One must be **conscientious** in one's work."

He hurried out with great strides in **agitation**, and pushed open the door of the machine room. He meticulously checked all the parts he had been working on during the day, until finally he was satisfied. "At last!" he said, "I can put my mind at ease." He wiped the sweat from his brow, and, with a sigh of relief, looked at his watch. It was nearly four o'clock. He pulled over from his desk an office chair, covered himself with an old blanket, and was soon asleep.

This was a normal scene in the daily routine of Hu Shuangqian, a senior technician at the **Shanghai Aircraft Manufacturing Co., Ltd.** He is known as the "Aviation **Craftsman**". Now fifty-five years old, Hu has been engaged in his profession for thirty-five years, and has worked on hundreds of thousands of airplanes without making a single mistake or offering a single **substandard** product. Asked about his birthday wish, Hu's face lights up as he says, "To contribute more to China's big airplanes for another ten or twenty years."

(397 words)

Checklist

1=Least Confident 2=Somewhat Confident 3=Extremely Confident

Learning Outcome Checklist	1	2	3
I am familiar with rising-falling intonation.			
I get familiar with loss of plosion.			
I can talk about employment security.			
The language of my presentation is correct and clear.			
I can retell the Chinese story *Search for Perfection*.			

5

Unit 5

Social Responsibility

Learning Focus

单元内容	Enjoying English	1）断句 2）连读 3）名言与绕口令 4）歌曲：*Heal the World* 拯救世界
	Testing Your Ears	1）慈善捐款 2）慈善集资 3）公益广告
	Talking Together	1）慈善 2）志愿活动
	Training Task	1）慈善 2）公益
	China Story	*Tu Youyou* 屠呦呦
单元目标	语言知识目标	能够用英语描述企业社会责任
	语言技能目标	1）能够听懂与企业社会责任相关的对话 2）能够用英语谈论企业社会责任
	学习策略	先捕捉大意，再关注细节
	情感态度	学习劳动者的劳动精神、奉献精神
	文化意识	讲中国故事，传播中医文化，增强民族自豪感
	职业素养	培养崇尚劳动、热爱劳动、辛勤劳动、诚实劳动的精神

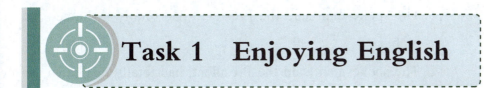

Task 1 Enjoying English

Part 1

Pauses

任务内容	辨析断句
任务目的	能够准确地断句
任务形式	听，回答，小组讨论
训练技能	利用不同断句位置表达不同意义

Directions: You will hear eight sentences. After each sentence, there will be a pause of ten seconds. During the pause, circle the letter next to the sentence you hear. The sentences will be spoken only once.

1. a. "John," explained Susan, "was in the classroom."
   b. John explained, "Susan was in the classroom."
2. a. Have we met Mr. Smith?
   b. Have we met, Mr. Smith?
3. a. John didn't accept it, because of Mary.
   b. John didn't accept it because of Mary.
4. a. What's two plus four, times three?
   b. What's two plus four times three?
5. a. I'm taking English history and art.
   b. I'm taking English, history and art.

6. a. Make sure to call, Paul.
   b. Make sure to call Paul.
7. a. The spokesman said the President had totally neglected the problem.
   b. The spokesman, said the President, had totally neglected the problem.
8. a. Can you hear Mr. Smith?
   b. Can you hear, Mr. Smith?

Part 2

Sentence Liaison

任务内容	辨析句子连读
任务目的	听懂并学会句子连读
任务形式	听，回答，小组讨论
训练技能	句子连读技巧

Directions: You will hear ten sentences which are already written out for you. Listen carefully and mark each case of liaison you hear. After you have finished marking, repeat what you hear. Each sentence will be read twice.

Example: What~is~it?

1. That's a piece of good news for him.
2. Why not go over for a visit?
3. I've been out and bought a paper.
4. I waited and waited for a bus.
5. How can I get to the railway station?
6. What do you think of it?

7. Art is long. Life is short.

8. East or west, home is best.

9. Where there is a will, there is a way.

10. A good beginning makes a good ending.

Proverbs and Tongue Twisters

（1）Proverbs

任务内容	学习名言警句
任务目的	从名言中获得启迪
任务形式	熟读，背诵
训练技能	启智增慧

Directions: Read the following proverbs after the recording and practice more by yourself.

Great minds think alike.

英雄所见略同。

Good things never come easy.

好事多磨。

He who has a mind to beat his dog will easily find a stick.

欲加之罪，何患无辞？

Losers are always in the wrong.

胜者为王，败者为寇。

（2）Tongue Twisters

任务内容	练习绕口令
任务目的	提升口语流利度
任务形式	自主练习，小组竞赛
训练技能	听音、辨音和发音能力

Directions: Read the following tongue twisters after the recording and practice more by yourself.

A noisy noise annoys an oyster.

嘈杂的噪声惹恼牡蛎。

A bloke's back bike brake block broke.

一个家伙的脚踏车后制动器坏了。

A box of biscuits, a batch of mixed biscuits.

一盒饼干，一批混合饼干。

A big black bug bit a big black bear, made the big black bear bleed blood.

一只黑色的大臭虫咬了一只黑色的大狗熊，大狗熊流血了。

A pleasant place to place a plaice is a place where a plaice is pleased to be placed.

放置鲽鱼最好的地方是鲽鱼愿意被放置的地方。

Part

Enjoy Yourself

Directions: Listen to the song and sing along.

Heal the World 拯救世界

There's a place in your heart

在你心中有个地方

And I know that it is love

我知道那里充满了爱

And this place could be much brighter than tomorrow

这个地方会比明天更灿烂

And if you really try

如果你真的努力过

You'll find there's no need to cry

你会发觉不必哭泣

In this place you'll feel

在这个地方

There's no hurt or sorrow

你感觉不到伤痛或烦忧

There are ways to get there

到那个地方的方法很多

If you care enough for the living

如果你真心关怀生者

Make a little space

营造一些空间

Make a better place...

创造一个更美好的地方……

Heal the world

拯救这世界

Make it a better place

让它变得更好

For you and for me and the entire human race

为你、为我，为了全人类

There are people dying

有人濒临死亡

If you care enough for the living

如果你真心关怀生者

Make a better place for you and for me
为你、为我，创造一个更美好的世界

If you want to know why
如果你想知道缘由

There's a love that cannot lie
因为爱不会说谎

Love is strong
爱是坚强的

It only cares of joyful giving
爱就是心甘情愿的奉献

If we try
若我们用心去尝试

We shall see
我们就会明白

In this bliss
只要心里有爱

We cannot feel fear or dread
我们就感受不到恐惧与忧虑

We stop existing
我们不再只是活着

And start living
而是真正开始生活

Then it feels that always
那爱的感觉将持续下去

Love's enough for us growing
爱让我们不断成长

So make a better world
去创造一个更美好的世界

Make a better world...
去创造一个更美好的世界……

Heal the world
拯救这世界

Make it a better place
让它变得更好

For you and for me and the entire human race
为你、为我,为了全人类

There are people dying
有人濒临死亡

If you care enough for the living
如果你真心关怀生者

Make a better place for you and for me
为你、为我,创造一个更美好的世界

And the dream we were conceived in
我们心中的梦想

Will reveal a joyful face
让我们露出笑脸

And the world we once believed in
我们曾经信赖的世界

Will shine again in grace
会再次闪烁祥和的光芒

Then why do we keep strangling life
那么我们为何仍在扼杀生命

Wound this earth
伤害地球

Crucify its soul
扼杀它的灵魂

Though it's plain to see
虽然这很容易明白

This world is heavenly be God's glow
这世界沐浴着圣人的荣光

Notes

We could fly so high

我们可以在高空飞翔

Let our spirits never die

让我们的精神不灭

In my heart I feel you are all my brothers

在我心中，你我都是兄弟

Create a world with no fear

共同创造一个没有恐惧的世界

Together we'll cry happy tears

我们一起流下喜悦的泪水

See the nations turn their swords into plowshares

看到许多国家把刀剑变成了犁耙

We could really get there

我们真的能达到梦想

If you cared enough for the living

只要你足够关怀生者

Make a little space

留个小小的空间

To make a better place...

创造一个更美好的世界……

Heal the world

拯救这世界

Make it a better place

让它变得更好

For you and for me and the entire human race

为你、为我，为了全人类

There are people dying

有人濒临死亡

If you care enough for the living

只要你足够关怀生者

Make it a better place for you and for me
为你、为我，创造一个更美好的世界

Heal the world
拯救这世界

Make it a better place
让它变得更好

For you and for me and the entire human race
为你、为我，为了全人类

There are people dying
有人濒临死亡

If you care enough for the living
只要你足够关怀生者

Make it a better place for you and for me
为你、为我，创造一个更美好的世界

Heal the world
拯救这世界

Make it a better place
让它变得更好

For you and for me and the entire human race
为你、为我，为了全人类

There are people dying
有人濒临死亡

If you care enough for the living
只要你足够关怀生者

Make it a better place for you and for me
为你、为我，创造一个更美好的世界

There are people dying
有人濒临死亡

If you care enough for the living
只要你足够关怀生者

Make it a better place for you and for me
为你、为我，创造一个更美好的世界

There are people dying
有人濒临死亡

If you care enough for the living
只要你足够关怀生者

Make it a better place for you and for me
为你、为我，创造一个更美好的世界

You and for me (make a better place)
为了你，我（创造一个更好的世界）

You and for me (make a better place)
为了你，我（创造一个更好的世界）

You and for me (make a better place)
为了你，我（创造一个更好的世界）

You and for me (heal the world we're living)
为了你，我（拯救我们生存的世界）

You and for me (save it for our children)
为了你，我（为了我们的孩子拯救世界）

You and for me (heal the world we're living)
为了你，我（拯救我们生存的世界）

You and for me (save it for our children)
为了你，我（为了我们的孩子拯救世界）

You and for me (heal the world we're living)
为了你，我（拯救我们生存的世界）

You and for me (save it for our children)
为了你，我（为了我们的孩子拯救世界）

You and for me (heal the world we're living)
为了你，我（拯救我们生存的世界）

You and for me (save it for our children)
为了你，我（为了我们的孩子拯救世界）

Task 2 Testing Your Ears

New Words

charity	n.	慈善
starving	adj.	饥饿的
donation	n.	捐赠物
deductible	adj.	可扣除的,可减免的
sponsor	v.	赞助
pledge	v.	保证给予
exposure	n.	亮相,被报道
billboard	n.	（大幅的）广告牌

Charitable Contributions

任务内容	关于慈善捐款的对话
任务目的	学会用英语讨论企业慈善行为
任务形式	听，填词
职场技能	联络与公关能力

Directions: Listen to the following dialogue twice and fill in the blanks.

A: Hello, my name is Peter. I'm calling on behalf of the Save the Children Fund. Have you heard of our (1)_____ before?

B: Um...yes, I think so. Don't you do some kind of charity work, like taking (2)_____ of starving children in Africa or something?

A: Yes, sir, that's exactly. We don't only (3)_____ the children in Africa, but we also take care of children in poverty all over the globe. Well, sir, I'm calling today to ask for your (4)_____ to our charitable organization.

B: Is that right?

A: We're a service organization that is a legally registered charity. We operate in more than a hundred countries, but most of our administration and workers are all volunteers. When you contribute to our cause, one hundred percent of your donation goes directly to the children who need it.

B: What kind of contribution are you asking for?

A: We accept donations of any amount, depending on your ability and desire to (5)_____. We can accept donations any where from twenty dollars to more than a thousand dollars. Additionally, your contribution is completely tax deductible. Can I count on you for support this year?

B: Sure, I'm willing to support your cause. How can I make a donation?

Fund-raising

任务内容	关于筹集慈善基金的对话
任务目的	能够用英语讨论慈善筹款活动
任务形式	听，填短语
职场技能	组织协调能力

Directions: *Listen to the following dialogue and fill in the blanks.*

A: How did your company's fund-raising go?

B: The fund-raising events went really well. We were able to (1)_____a few of our competitors, all in fun, of course, to sponsor a marathon for the American Cancer Society. All of the people who participated it (2)_____, and we were able to raise a lot of money (3)_____to cancer research.

A: So how does it work? How were you able to make money with the marathon?

B: Each of the runners that participated the marathon race paid a ten dollar entrance fee. Also, they went (4)_____to get sponsors who pledged a dollar per mile that participants ran. (5)_____we were able to raise several thousand dollars.

A: Sounds like a great deal for the American Cancer Society.

B: In all honesty, it's also a great deal for our company. The exposure that we gained from sponsoring an invent like this was great for our image in the community. We accomplished as much as last year's advertising campaign, plus we were able to do a little fund-raising for a good cause.

Notes

Part 3

Public Service Advertisement

任务内容	关于公益广告的对话
任务目的	能够用英语讨论公益广告的社会功能
任务形式	听，填句子
职场技能	语言表达能力

Directions: Listen to the following dialogue twice and fill in the blanks.

A: What do you think about the public service advertisement for quitting smoking?

B: While I think it's great that they're trying to get people to quit smoking, but I don't really care for the advertisement.

B: (1) _____?

A: The fish hook that they use is quite disturbing!

B: (2) _____. They use the fish hook to make you think about how you can get "hooked" on smoking.

A: I know, but I think it's not really appropriate for young children.

B: I think they're trying to scare the young people (3) _____.

A: All advertisers like to catch young people because they know the meaning of loyalty.

B: (4) _____, though. Maybe the advertisement would be more effective with adults anyhow.

A: I have nothing against them putting the advertisements in magazines and newspapers that are read by adults, but I don't think they should have their ads on billboards where children can see them.

B: (5) _____. I think I was so delighted to see that a billboard was being used to promote health that I didn't think about how children might understand the ads.

A: You have to give them credit, though. It's about time people started becoming more aware of the dangers of smoking.

Task 3   Talking Together

New Words

fund	n.	资金
rating	n.	等级,评价
cruelty	n.	残忍,虐待
expertise	n.	专长
remote	adj.	遥远的,偏远的
gallery	n.	画廊

Part 1

Charity

任务内容	关于企业慈善行为的对话
任务目的	学会用英语讨论企业慈善行为
任务形式	角色扮演
职场技能	协调能力

Conversation 1:

Directions: Complete the following dialogue according to the hints given in Chinese and role-play it with your partner.

A: The recommendation is that 60% of funds should go to projects with (1)_____ (不多于) 40% going to the charity's own costs.

M: Here's another good website: Charity Navigator.org. You can search specific groups and check their ratings. Red Cross is number five in the "Most Recommended Charities".

G: There's also animal-related groups. (2)_____ (怎么样) the Society for the Prevention of Cruelty to Animals?

F: They're number four on the list. (3)_____ (听起来不错).

J: World Vision is number one. They're a Christian group that provides lot of medical assistance in Asia and Africa.

M: And of course, while we all enjoy doing a good deed, we do need to ensure that the company can get a tax break from our contributions.

G: I'll double check that donations to each of those groups are (4)_____ (事实上) tax-deductible.

F: I just had a thought. Every year we give corporate donations and that's all well and good, but we might consider giving our time instead.

G: Interesting! You mean like volunteering? I like it.

M: Hummm... that could work. Any specific suggestions?

F: Well, we all have our pet causes. Gina is an animal lover. I have church projects. Jenny is a computer genius. We all have something we could teach or offer.

J: That idea is very worth considering. (5)_____ (从某些角度). That's a lot more meaningful than giving money.

M: OK, how about if we give half of our contribution as donations and for the other half we give our time or expertise to the group of our choice?

All: Agree!

Part 2

Volunteering

任务内容	关于志愿活动的对话
任务目的	能够用英语讨论志愿活动
任务形式	角色扮演
职场技能	履行社会责任

Conversation 2:

Directions: Place the following sentences in correct order to form a dialogue and role-play it with your partner.

a. How did you come up with the idea of volunteering?

b. Was it a full-time job for him?

c. So you mean volunteering is not just donating cash or things?

d. For me, it's not only a choice, but a responsibility.

e. I'd like to join you someday.

A: Hello. Peter. I heard you worked in a remote village last month.

B: Yes, as a volunteer teaching in a primary school in southeastern China.

A: A good choice for the summer vacation.

B: (1) _____

A: You're right. What can a volunteer generally do?

B: Many things, like creating a change in the surroundings, providing shelter and food to

the needy ones.

A: (2)_____

B: Right! We prefer to call that charity.

A: (3)_____

B: It was my father. He used to supervise a volunteer program in a non-profit art gallery.

A: (4)_____

B: No, in fact a part-time job. He went to the gallery nearly every weekend.

A: Wow. This requires great passion.

B: Sure. The best way to volunteer is to get involved in activities we are passionate about.

A: Have you had any difficulties as a volunteer?

B: Definitely! Lack of respect, acknowledgement, and lack of funds now and then.

A: Oh, my! Many obstacles!

B: So the most important spirit is perseverance.

A: (5)_____

B: Any time.

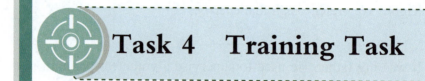

Task 4　Training Task

任务内容	1）慈善 2）公益
任务目的	能够用英语讨论慈善与公益
任务形式	角色扮演
职场技能	从事慈善行为与参加公益活动的能力

Directions: *Make dialogues for the following situations. You can refer to the words, expressions and patterns given below.*

Situation 1: *The two employees of a company are talking about the charity matter. Please make up a dialogue and act it out with your partners.*

Reference:

contribution; voluntary contribution; donation（to sb./sth.）

to make a donation to charity; a generous/large/small donation; organ donation; give sth. away

We rely entirely on voluntary contribution.

Would you like to make a donation to the Women's and children's hospital?

Billionaires in various countries are increasingly putting more of their money into charity.

Situation 2: *Two students are discussing volunteering. Please make up a dialogue and act it out with your partners.*

Reference:

Our class had a public benefit activity.

We went to nursing homes to recite English and Chinese texts and sing songs for the old ladies and men.

We read a text about the loneliness of the people in the nursing homes.

So we are volunteering to hold this volunteer labor. We have prepared our own part for a week.

We brought our performance there and showed them one by one.

The old were laughed happily, so did we.

It's so good to have such activity.

Task 5　China Story

New Words

artemisinin	n.	青蒿素
malaria	n.	疟疾
anonymously	adv.	不知名地
pharmacologist	n.	药物学家
extraction	n.	提炼
laurel	n.	荣誉

Directions: Read the story and try to retell it.

任务内容	屠呦呦的故事
任务目的	用英语传播中医文化
任务形式	英语复述
职场技能	语言描述能力

Tu Youyou

Tu Youyou won the 2015 Nobel Prize for the discovery of **artemisinin**, a drug that is now the top treatment for **malaria**. Tu has risked her life in her dedication to finding a cure for malaria. For decades, she worked almost **anonymously** before winning the Nobel Prize in 2015.

"Ancient Chinese medicine has valuable treasure. We should work hard to tap into the rich resources in it. Artemisinin was discovered from it. Through research, I find that Chinese medicine and western medicine each has its own advantages and can be complementary to each other. Proper combination of the two will generate bigger potentials in medical development."

Born in 1930, Tu Youyou suffered from a lung disease when she was young, but Chinese medicine saved her life. She developed a keen interest in traditional Chinese medicine, dedicating her life to being a **pharmacologist**.

The achievement didn't come easy. Tu explains that her discoveries were made after years of repeated tries and failures.

"I experimented on over 200 kinds of Chinese medicines and I tried about 380 **extraction** methods in total. They all failed. I named my starting point as No. 91, because I found the effective component after 191 experiments."

To ensure that the drug would be safe in humans, at one time Tu even tested the medicine on her own.

"I was determined to find the effects of the medicine that year. I made a report to ask for permission to test the drug on myself. I was the team leader and took the responsibility. Some of my colleagues also participated in the program. We went into Dongzhimen Hospital for the test."

Jiang Tingliang is former President of the Institute of Chinese Materia Medica of the Academy of Chinese Medical Sciences. He says he was impressed by Tu's strong determination in conducting her research.

"I was impressed by her persistence in her work and scientific research, without which she couldn't have made such remarkable achievements. She'd been persistent from the very beginning."

Tu Youyou also won China's top science award in 2017 for her outstanding contributions to scientific and technological innovation. But she didn't rest on her **laurels** after winning these awards. She continued to work at perfecting her discoveries.

(389 words)

Checklist

1=Least Confident　　　　2=Somewhat Confident　　　　3=Extremely Confident

Learning Outcome Checklist	1	2	3
I am familiar with the pauses.			
I get familiar with the phenomenon of sentence liaison.			
I can make communications about the topics of charity and volunteering.			
The language of my presentation is correct and clear.			
I can retell the Chinese story of *Tu Youyou*.			